QUIET, GRI

Ra

ISBN: 978-1-913642-28-0

Book designed by Aaron Kent

Edited by Aaron Kent

Broken Sleep Books (2020), Talgarreg, Wales

Contents

Quiet, Grit, Glory

Ricky Ray

To care for what we know
requires care for what we don't,
the world's lives dark in the soil,
dark in the dark.

—*Wendell Berry*

Pain: 8 on a Scale of 10

Some days, I never make it out of my head, that coal-eyed melon
where all my dreams crumble and drift into the weeds of Styx.

The impinged nerves crack their whips within my animal pelt.
My tongue plays dead in my mouth, afraid of how much more

it would hurt to cry out. But some cries cannot be stifled. Some hurts
have to get worse before they get better. If they get better—*if*.

Some nights, the sleeve of me seizes and I hear in my writhing
the devil's laugh. He's a son of a bitch, but I don't even have enough

left in me to hate him. Let him have this. Let him gnaw me
past care and bone. There's nothing here but hurt,

and I don't want it. I want to close the eyes of my eyes,
stuff the blown world in a sack, throw it over my shoulder

and slip between two ticks of the pulse, leaving
all the arguments of the flesh to cancel one another out.

Varieties of Service

Driving home through the green hills of Vermont, I couldn't help feeling attacked. Words like wasps circling and stinging my mind. Attacked for my faults, my failures, for how little I made of my life. A little that seems like so much from within. It's good to be stung, to think of the hive, of the queen, of the servants and their many heads. The bites were tender, sore, and the way I touched them reminded me to be quiet in my thoughts. Gentle in my acts. To touch soft as a stray petal that lands like luck in my glove.

Addie settles into new places quickly. Owns them. Barks at intruders, readies herself to leap over the desk out the window at the skunk. I could call her to heel but what for? She could hurt herself. Oh, let her quiver with the thought of the catch. She deserves it. She's growing old, slowing down the way wilderness wilts. I am no more her master than I am the master of myself. We serve each other. Our wills are two countries with their own customs but no clearly defined border. In that co-existence, she knows the language of my hands better than I know it myself. And I know her upper lip tucked under her lower canine when curiosity crinkles the tip of her nose, and mischief marches towards the knots of her paws.

My wife sees the worry in my face and says I'm too sensitive, softens it and says I'm too kind. This from the woman who fretted over the ant that hitchhiked into her office, the woman who used her lunch hour to return the poor speck to the park. Wishing him reunited with his tribe. I wonder what happens to a lost ant and remind her, though she never believes me, though she often is what she disbelieves, that when it comes to sensitivity, and when it comes to kindness, there is no such thing as enough.

Into the Dark

Every year the cherry trees *fatten with brag*.
Every year we return.

Addie presses her nose into my palm for a treat.
On each kernel of popcorn:

the scent of my heart:
raw in my hand, she'd eat it with haste.

I hate cold days but pray for them
so I can watch her sparkle in the nip.

The daggers of my spine come for me,
and she rests her head in my lap to soften the stab.

Her worn teeth make me wince.
I check the grey in her muzzle and wish it back.

I rehearse her death in my mind too often.
I'm rehearsing my own death in hers.

I don't want to go before her.
I want her nose—the chocolate nose

that can lift into the air and scan
the placement and history and hurt of everything—

to smell my hand on her head
as she closes her eyes, and closes her heart,

and I let myself follow her
into the dark.

Resolution

For 18 years, my new year's resolution
has been to publish a book. Cross that one
off the list. Now what do I do with myself?

The lights in the hallway still don't work.
My body keeps auditioning to play the part of a poem.
Doesn't it know how bad I am at revising,

how I throw away more poems than I fix,
how I write reams of rubbish and generally
flub my way into moments of luck?

And it wants the part? Listen, body,
I'm not very good at this. But it's snowing.
And the mind is beautiful when she's quiet.

And if you're lonely in that spinal hell, know
that I spent most of those 18 years oiling your gears,
massaging your joints and ordering ointments,

believing in magic, that old byproduct of song.
Body, I hear you singing to yourself sometimes,
and I cry. Keep singing, friend, and if,

when you come to the end of your years,
you hear a little roar and wonder what that noise is,
I'll tell you: it's the sound of me cheering you on.

Inconstancy

Isn't your average mutt a mix of six righteous whiskies?
Or is the taste of dumb living always barbed wire

strung down the middle of your gut? I couldn't rightly say.
I speak so wrong truth's a creature rarely encountered.

But it lingers this side of myth. It watches from the trees.
I sleep with it, some nights. It fits like a bone

that doesn't break, or if it breaks, it's just a mouthful
of bread. One day and the next offer such contrary

weathers, it's hard to know how to take them.
The stomach might color everything nauseous

or the joints might grind like gears wearing each other out
or the little harmony that visits your chest

a couple of times each swing of the moon might just
set up a band between your ears and tap its toes all day.

The Rabid Breeding of Yeses

for Barbara Henning

Lost—the streets crotchsour—hacking addict—dogs circle—
sniff one end to the other—Johnny says New York gurgled
like a tar pit in his bones—but his nights—never moving
past the halfway skip in the record—her hair fought the air—
Spanish moss—sweaty temple—two months' breath—
bye bye baby—bathing in Mississippi bathtub bourbon—
sky blue dead hue—I buy marrow—$5 a pound—
no poem so hard as a femur—if time loses itself as I sit
in the breaking beauty of my body—can forever recover
from a cold sip of never—whatever—what is music
if not the rabid breeding of yeses—no other—even hope
is excessive—Eliot was right—life not given but lent.

The What of Us

I

The idea that someone lives here
gives birth to the illusion of who I am:
Ricky Ray. Nigh on forty.
Broke and broken.
Suspicious of anthropes.
Lover of dogs.
A muddle of music, morals and blood.

I have chosen to be human
more days than I wish to admit.
I have chosen animality too few.
The canary of my courage
clutches my clavicle
and pecks at the emotions I offer its beak.

The idea that somebody
lives here: a false coat.
The body lives,
and something, not someone,
picks the spine up in the morning
and feeds the mouth bananas
and puts the head down
on the pillow at night.

II

Many little bodies inhabit each body like a nest.
Each body inhabits a larger body like a nest.

I hear you in there.
Do you hear me in you?

We share what we are,
what lives us, what is us.

It wears everything.
It wears everything out.

We want to name it.
Language issues from our bones

and the ground
and the invisible indivisible that wants to be said.

(Or so we say,
coloring the quiet with desire.)

III

It warms the mouth.

It looks in the mirror and sees the ghost
of every man, woman and child who made me.
The ghost of every animal,
mineral and element who made them.

It sees the ghost of the last male
in the Ray line
childless by a choice so hard
the tears shatter my sight like glass.

IV

One day, I will tell you why,
but for now, this branch
of the family tree bears no leaf
in preparation for falling away.
Turning brittle. Breaking off.

And yet, how many sticks
have I thrown,
have my dog Addie mouthed
from the ground in love?

There's hope in it
I can't explain.

The tree reaches toward the light
until it too falls over
from too many riches.

That which lives us
unselves us, unveils us:
sweet revelation impales us.

How beautiful that *who*
was always a brief glimpse
into *what*.

Charlie

I

She saunters across the green hill in her feline faultlessness, then pauses, the sight of prey unfolding in her like a present unwrapped one layer of tissue at a time. Her steps become measured, mechanical, each footfall a calculation where to crinkle a leaf is to telegraph her intent. She drops low to the ground and time bends around her, her shoulder advancing like a sculpture pulling itself free from the rock.

The wind flattens the grass and the leaves chatter and the shrew parts the meadow in search of seed. Charlie can already taste its neck and twitches her ass, flattens her ears, sees it happen: the shrew's last-second awareness, the squeal, the attempt to flee, the pounce, the grab, the bite. And then she lives out the film she has already seen, graceful as water, if water were a snake that struck, flowing to the lowest level, the rapid pulse, the aphrodisiac of fear, the fangs sunk in the trembling throat.

If that were all, it would be fair, but the kill does not amuse the perpetual kitten. She releases and pounces, pounces and bites, tosses and bats and catches and drops. The shrew cries and bleeds and struggles and flees, first on a broken leg, then a torn open gut, then an eye that spills its jelly down the cheek. Charlie bites until breath is the shrew's only response, and loses interest. In boredom she leaves it to the fire of ants and the slow crawl of the sun.

II

I step into the late light and head to the barn, half-expecting the find. A storm pushes its black head across the horizon and I notice the scuffled grass. *Charlie. Again. Damnit.* I nudge the shrew with the toe of my boot and it lets out the barest squeak, so slight it could be the rub of my boot against the grass, but I bend down and see, through bloodslick grey, the slow rise and fall of its ribs. I close my eyes. I walk away. I come back. And again I bring down the shovel until the Earth is the shrew's new skin.

The rain falls. I spear the shovel and burn. What's done is done. The axe calls. I have wood to chop. A fire to build. A family to warm against winter's icy kisses on the backs of our necks. My heart's heaviness seems contained in the head of the axe. We have been here before. Too many times. I have held Charlie face down in what was left of the kill, cuffing her neck. She growled. I growled back.

I chop and stack, work up a sweat. The cracks echo like gunshots through the woods. Every so often, I stop and call out to her, careful to control my tone. Waiting for her to show her face. Around about dusk, the rain lets up and she pokes her head through the door of the barn. I smile and speak sweetly, coaxing, soothing. She approaches and watches me lift the hatchet from my belt.

Drying Out

The dog comes in from the rain
and shakes, droplets
flying in every direction,
then stretches out against the stove—

so it is with betrayal:
I molt you from my limbs,
but I'm still wet with you
and will be a long time drying.

Varieties of Help

Addie has a nose for injured birds.
We nurse them to one version of the sky
or its wingless other. And the pups
she cannot have, and the kids we do not have,
flock in dreams that rise like premonitions:
pick something sick, feed it, and if others
see its breath curl against the winter sky,
aren't we decent parents? In Sheepshead Bay
the ocean takes the corner of a house, promises
she'll be back. She's been known to lie before,
but there's arctic assurance in her vow.
The way the sparrows fill the forest
makes me wonder what my cells are singing.
My wife saves a drowning fly, hatches a plan:
hire mercenaries to mow down poachers.
If I weren't broken, if life hadn't stuck
its hand into the wiring of my nervous system
and yanked, I'd join her. We'd do one better.
We'd resurrect in ourselves a cross between
the saber-toothed cat and a pissed-off mammoth.
We'd fill the air with the blood-thick cries
of men who wanted to live—and die—by the hunt.

Yourself in Headlights

So what if you're a little drunk
and the car flies
like a bullet without a leash on it
until there's a thunk
underneath the Michelin tread
so you stop

and get out of the car
to carry the warm body
to the side of the road
where you smooth its torn mask
as its blood pools on the grass,
then you dig a hole with bare hands,

wishing you knew
how to use those hands
to put the raccoon and your life
back together. What if you had to pick one,
your life or the raccoon,
and the raccoon babies

were pleading with you to choose wisely
and your wife was pleading
with you to tell her it wasn't true
and your conscience
was pleading with you
to do the right thing…

But it's useless, it's all useless
so you shove your hands
into the river of its guts
and you tear the raccoon apart,
and then you lift them
into the beams of light,

tempted to lick your fingers clean
thinking
she loves me rabies
she loves me not
but at the right angle
they catch the light and glisten,

and you stop
and think:
one day,
years from now,
it might all
begin to make sense.

from *Working Definitions*

Substitution

For a decade I watched the wind
shred the plastic bag on the fire escape
because there were no trees.

Dread

These shadows passing—
are they birds of prey
or whole days I stayed in bed?

Adaptation

I cut the carrot with my teeth—bite and spit,
bite and spit—because my shoulders
are too ruined to cut it with a knife.

Ache

I want a poem so close to hurt
it bruises my lips on the way out.

Providence

Somewhere on a boardwalk in Rhode Island,
as August drops every pooch
in a state of stupor,
the boiled ocean condenses
in the sky and falls
into the mouth of the man too drunk
to rise. What drove him there,
where the worms push
out of the wet Earth
and the man burrows
so far into himself
his liver shivers as if afraid
to acknowledge where he's gone?

> (In that far interior, the cocktail
> of blood and bourbon
> crashes like waves
> against the bruise-colored rocks.
> What's left of the man—
> a faint light hovering in Irish mist—
> approaches the limits of the body's music:
> hearing itself becomes pure tone.
> He watches a robin weave
> a strand of plastic into her nest;
> she finds comfort
> in the rustle it makes
> while the wind tries to tear her apart.)

Meanwhile, the clouds clear
and the sun splits the man's lips
until the knife of light
cuts too far
and he stumbles back
to the windows of consciousness,
vomits on the fact of himself,

blood on his hand from the attempt
to wipe the sting away.
Instantly the tongue greets
its old friend iron
and the man begs them all
to keep quiet.

      No whistling for weeks.
      Wheezing enough to dance to.
      Who says sin isn't sexy?
      Or a reliable rhythm?
      Do it right
      and regret's merely
      the slow-
      motion
      out-
      tide of fate
      reversing as the hand
      reaches towards the dice
      and fingers them into its palm.

His last ten dollars on the line,
which he doesn't have,
which he'll pay for
with a blowjob if he loses,
the man sucks on the vine of breath
as if in preparation for prayer.
He speaks to the dice
as into the ear of God,
calls them his wooden tadpoles,
kisses their six eyes,
thinks of them as the eyes of flies,
their wings
the weight of wonder
if he could dig it from his bones.

      He shakes them twice
      and blows for luck,
      lips burning with a taunt
      as he snaps his wrist and rolls:
      '

come on God—kitty's hungry—
baby's burning—
we need a little sign of forgiveness—
tease the trout—
place two more dollars
on the eyes of the oracle—
sew her mouth shut—
get off your great invisible ass
and provide.

Continuity in the Park

For my pleasure as much as hers,
    I scratch Addie just below the ears
        and her eyes half close
and she looks at me as if we were made for this. We were.
    It feels cold to me, just right to her,
        so I scooch closer to steal her warmth.

She licks the thin film of peanut butter
    from the tip of my finger
        and I almost want to be the nut,
to become her, to fuel her,
    if only the fuel she'll use to turn
        her other side towards the sun.

Then I want to be the light. These are the times
    when I hear the Earth singing us into existence.
        Arthritis lays me down in the grass.
An oriole stops to consider its business.
    There are poems that have no words.
        I am living one this minute.

This morning, Addie barked at a man
    who knocked at our door,
        and now someone who lived
in this sentience before me, before it was mine,
    before there were houses and doors,
        has found his way back.

He reminds me that Addie and I once slept
    in earlier hides around small fires,
        her ears scanning the skies
while she chased down prey in her sleep,
    her rough voice my only warning
        of predators approaching us in the dark.

So I trust in Addie's bark and the dark
    and the fact that we will live
        in as many forms as many times
as there are bodies to be woven—
    she will become my human and I her dog
        who rests his head in her lap and drifts to sleep.

Passivity Is a Recipe for Dust

She asked for both hands. Inspected them with her fingers, as if my health were written in Braille on my wrists and she could read it. She said she *could hardly detect a pulse.* I seemed to be alive and lifted my eyebrows. *Not your heart pulse,* she said, *one of the others—there are four. And the missing pulse is the pulse of the ego.* I smiled, said *yes, it was hard work, scrubbing me out.* She shook her head, looked sad. Said *no, you need to leave a little; desire's an essential oil; otherwise you're bound to dry out.*

Once in Twelve Years, I Go to Church

I go to the church with the cross in it
and I kneel, because it hurts too much to sit,
and I pray, wordlessly. I go when it's quiet,
when service is over, ideally when no one
is there. But someone is always there.

I don't mean the priest. I don't mean Jesus
or some deity who looks down on us.
God does not look down on us.
God does not exist, and yet God is
all there is. I mean I look at these walls,

mammoth two-foot by four-foot
blocks of limestone that could crush us,
beautifully. And I recall that limestone
is composed entirely of skeletal fragments,
of organisms caught in their less-than-final

resting places. And I hear in the stone
a rustling, the rustling of creatures
who once crept and bled upon the Earth,
like you and me. Creatures still here,
still whispering in our ears, still embodied

and participating in the language of the world.
What I hear is: that word—*upon*—is wrong.
We say *upon* as if the Earth were merely
lithosphere—the ground beneath—
and not the atmosphere, the Ecosphere:

not the sky and why above, not the blood
and good within. We say *upon* as if
the Earth and men were not each other,
and the lesser was merely a visitor
upon the greater's soils. We say *upon*

but mean as one, we mean the Earth
rose up and lived as us, as she lives
the creatures who whisper in these walls,
and as she lives the little poet
turning to limestone in this poem.

Self-Portrait in Crayola, Yeast and Violets

I

Green and red, blue. What else do I need?
Black, I need night in the box of crayons
sucking every color into itself the way
despair sucks every breath out of the room.

II

Everyone I ever met swims in me
whether I want them to or not.
Desire, permission, fondness, indifference
seem beside the point—my membership resides,
becoming different people in me
than they are in their own bodies.

Sometimes I prefer my version to the real thing.
Sometimes they improve me against my will,
coloring the portrait I respond to in the mirror,
working their hands in my dough.

III

What kind of bread am I? Pumpernickel, rye.
Dense, texture that recalls the dirt it came from, seedy,
a lump slowly passing down the mysteries of the throat.

Soaked in broth that simmers for three days, I crumble,
an ode to dissolution, a flower that wants the light
to bend back its petals until they leave the nest and fly.

They won't make it far. But far enough
to leap from the ledge of their old life and fall.

V

For a couple of hours, I'll remember
the pattern they made against the ground,
but like everything else I swore to love,
the memory will fade so fast
I'll wonder who's emptying me out,

and all I'll be left with—a great gift—
is a faint impression of how seeing the pattern felt.

When You Call

Answering to my name isn't enough.
I have to prepare the person
you expect to meet when he opens the door.

It's a difficult task. He's here
the way breath is, the way the past is,
but so is the Earth, the Universe,

gypsy jazz and radicchio,
and to fold them down into the size of a man
isn't something I'm good at.

It all fits poorly, bulges, leaks,
and I like the leaks so much,
the music they make, I don't want to talk;

I want to listen through you:
to hear what my ears alone
can't hear of our notes in the scale:

the sound of the spheres igniting us both.
Which is what talking is,
I suppose, but to converse,

while listening to the music
behind the talk we make,
requires me to construct someone

and put him in charge of the tongue.
Sometimes he disappears
and the mouth lapses into a silence

that stretches on and stretches on,
and you begin to wonder,
understandably, whether I'm all there.

Petty Theft

It started as baseball cards and candy bars.
Money from my father's wallet. Protein bars on a health kick.
Eventually my friends and I walked into a grocery store,
loaded up on beer and ice cream and walked out,
calm as day, as if being alive,
in need of sugar and stupefaction was payment enough.
When I drove across the country and ran out of money,
I'd approach a state line, fill up and haul ass,
believing the trooper couldn't book me on his neighbor's turf.
I was lucky, never arrested. Never shot. Never killed.
Once or twice I stole a heart. *That* fucked me up —
as soon as I had it in my hands I wanted to put it back,
but you couldn't *do that* without hurting the person you took it from.
Later, it was clothes from thrift stores,
a book from a writing center inscribed by one of my holy influences —
monsieur Valery — a theft I'm most proud of, I'll never repent.
A girlfriend goaded me into my lowest:
CDs from my father's truck,
which I pawned for a couple of bucks a pop — music,
the one thing in my father's life that wasn't drugs,
depression and skull-crushing drudgery —
the theft I wish amongst my deepest wishes that I could take back.
A little time on the clock, you bet.
Then karma played her hand: her dirty hand:
my identity was lifted one night from my pocket,
drunk, asleep on the train.
My reincarnation was a bastard,
stole a dog and a car, got slapped with a felony,
used my social security number to tarnish my good name.
As long as he had good cause and took good care of the dog,
I wish him good health.
If not, may an intestinal parasite gut him to death.
I worked and I stole, more of one than the other.
Which? Depended on the day.
Somewhere along the way I formed a philosophy:

earning is good, finding is better,
sharing the best, belonging the bestest:
nothing I ever loved was purely the product of money or theft,
and nothing I ever touched belonged to me more than I belonged to it
and it to the belonging in which all things fight and make up.
To be at home in the Earth's pocket, where I've always been,
a unicorn nugget, collecting lint, casting sparks,
to realize that, and feel it—
what else could an old thief want?

Walk with Addie

Addie found the strange scat full of fish scales again, found it on the peninsula where the beavers murder the trees, shearing the bark, the sap rolling down the exposed wood like tears. Addie found it and, unlike the deer and goose poop she gobbles faster than I can say no, this she wanted to roll in, to embed herself in the scales, the scat, the scent. Imagine being a creature with a nose so strong you could smell a piece of crust two hundred yards away, and being so enthralled by the waft of shit, your instinctual response is to enter it. She rolled and rolled, sneezing irrepressible sneezes of joy, then she stood and shook, and all of it fell.

She trotted on and I felt fortunate to be taught by her. To witness the embodiment of an infatuation one dives into like a second skin, then leaves behind, head down, already on the scent of the many infatuations ahead. I think I live in my head the way she lives in her nose. The way I roll around in the perfume of an idea, which slowly fades, the faint aroma lingering in my thoughts throughout the day. An idea like: we're helping the Earth know herself, and in exchange, she's gifting us intimacy, consciousness, the experience of being everything in sight. And in smell.

I'd like to live in the part of Addie that processes smell for an hour. The part that can read the air the way I hear the Earth thinking my thoughts, revealing the shape and scent of comprehension. The size of the beaver. The fish become scales. I close my eyes, wanting only to linger in this communion while I can. Addie and I climb a hill and sit on a rock overlooking Eureka Lake. Geese honk their little notes of gruel from the water. The Earth hands me a heartbeat and I hand Addie a treat and the way she eats it is gratitude. The way I watch her eat it is gratitude. The wind speaks and we nod. We talk of our hike and our fondness for each other without saying a word.

Family

At night, when Addie sniffs the snow for deer
and I sniff the smoke from the neighbor's
chimney for understanding,
                         I think the stars
out there are in here, under my ribs,
which are no longer mine but the body
of some great heaving that holds us
together,
            the one we were before the big
bang, and still are, radiating the universe
in the aftermath of birth,
entropy, loss,
                the slow effervescence
of heat leaking toward a winter
in which all hearts and stars go dark.

Dark: where the light begins.
When it began,
               the sun was a mote
in its beam, and us a blip in its mote,
and yet here we are,
                  devastating
a beautiful planet,
                  looking for reasons
to acknowledge our destruction
and the inevitability
                  of our undoing,
and still somehow concluding
that the correct response is love.

Which may include deciding
not to have children—the thing
I wanted most in this world.

Reasons for God #17

There's something about being alive
that makes us cry out for help.

Good Men Die and Mediocre Men Fill Their Shoes

for Gary Thomas

Good men die and mediocre men fill their shoes.
I wear one of each until the soles wear out
and then I wear my feet until the bones wear out
and then the Earth sews me into some other
specimen until she tires of this species of living,
of life as a species of being. She has other modes
to try. Every day I hurt so much I could implode
and teach the Universe a thing or two about suffering.
Or learn that suffering is the Universe's lesson
and my small share couldn't goosebump a mouse.

Of course my pain is relative, and yes, doctor,
you're entitled to falsify me, since we're related,
however strange, however estranged, and since
I love and hate you, whoever you are, like family.
We were born into each other. Brother to sister
and human to ant, or piss-ant, as the case
may be. If I bite you, doctor, and my venom
causes you to experience one day in the hell
that is my body, will you believe in *that*? I bet
you'd offer me a mainline into poppy puredom.

Ignore me. I'm drunk. A little tipsy, pleasantly
buzzed. A good man died today. You know him.
Your predecessor. The man whose shoes you
could swim laps in. He died two months ago
but I just received the news. He took care of me
until cancer took him down the alley called
the last six months of his life. I didn't know
he was so close, had no right to, thought I had
plenty of time to write him the letter I cannot
now write or deliver. What would I have said?

Thank you, Gary, you saved me, I survived
because of your magic hands. And then
I would have been selfish, whiny, I would have
complained that the man who has taken your place,
who tends to your patients, that pudgy pimple,
is an imbecile. That isn't fair, he's new at this,
and scared of the authorities, as well he
should be, dealing drugs. But his manner
is shifty, dishonest—I have proof, nevermind.

Gary, they should make them in your mold.
All physicians should know the body the way
your fingers hunted hurt in mine. Then shot it.
And when it dared rise up against me, you shot it
again. But since that letter cannot be written,
let me try this one: Gary, if I may, if two months of us
from the other side of the divide hasn't driven you
out of your mind, and out of this town—if you are,
and if you have a spare hour, come meet me where
doctors and patients check their formalities at the door.

Let it be your favorite bar. Let me buy you a drink.
Let me buy you ten. I'll pour them at what used to be
your mouth and you'll laugh at the puddle of bourbon
pooling under your bar-stool, and we'll speak
of the body's tendency to scream at itself
when it loses its shit as if the body it screamed at
wasn't the one doing the screaming, making it worse,
and at the end of the night I'll get down and lap up
the puddle, sloppily, like the drunk dog I am.

I'll even bark for you. But I won't hug you,
or harangue you with tears, or beg you for one
final script. God knows you don't want to smell me,
my agony, or my grief. I'll say so long, farewell
in doglish, maybe even lift my leg at you and let fly
with a wink of the eye, give you something to tell
the others as you stand in line to hand in your ghost
and go where good men go when they've had enough
of men and their moaning and their silly ideas of dying.

Low

Unable to do much of anything,
I ask for help and it doesn't come.

It comes but I'm too blinded
by self-pity to recognize it:

the will to breathe: a breath the wind
blows into my lungs to keep me going.

It wasn't that I was dying—
I was—but that the day seemed

hardly worth responding to, a lover
I couldn't muster the will to meet in bed.

I knew this a deficiency in me,
but that only turned the static up.

Redeeming the Invitations

So little snow it felt like bouts of dandruff salting the ground.
The lake froze, but even Addie's sixty-eight pounds broke through.
She sensed it happening, leaped from the cracking ice and landed

on the bank, tail carving the air. Seeing it, someone pulled the string
on the lightbulb in my chest. No wonder the ticks love her.
No wonder I follow her lead and rub my face in the snow,

would-be spontaneous but I'm selecting the medium: I don't have
the courage to rub it in dirt. She wakes me in the middle of the night
and I get up, groggy but glad to take her out. I'll complain in the morning

but I'm storing these moments as presents for when she's gone.
I'll take them out, sniff them over and cry. Who else would greet
the 3am wind like an old friend come to visit, throw herself into its arms?

Sleep is for the dead, she says, *there's more to this day than poems
and pie.* She's approaching eighty in dog years, but lives as if
she's thirty-five. I think it's partially for my benefit: she sees me

in her rearview, unsteady at the wheel, and knows she still has a lot
to teach me about aging, about ignoring it, about how to throw my body—
even when it fails me, even when it hurts like hell—headlong into joy.

How to Go On

Sometimes, when defeat
sits in your chest
sinking you past concern,

you have to lie down in a field,
look up at the sky,
and ask the blades of grass, the little Earthlings

who have been there all night,
who have lived there all their lives,
who are the field you are becoming,

to slip their slender green
fingers into your mind,
and show you:

To go on? It's easy:
you open your mouth,
you take in little sips of light.

Acknowledgements

Every poem is a child of many kindnesses. And hardships. And days spent turning sunlight into another kind of warmth. A warmth to hold against our oblivions. A warmth to add to our radiances. Every person who made each poem possible inheres in its brief light, and I think of them now, fondly, the ones I've known, and the ones I couldn't, as I consider this word—acknowledgment—and what it means to pay tribute. What it means to be grateful, to live in gratitude, to say I'm here, and I wrote these things (as well as I could), because I was the recipient of your kindness, because I am the recipient of you—you, kin, who helped me learn to read; and you, kin, who turned the creativity of the Earth, her autopoiesis thrumming in your blood, into language, into art, into a way to preserve and transmit understanding across time and distance. I am the recipient of you, my infinite teachers; and you, my foul-mouthed detractors; you, the indifferent throng; and you, the fire-tailed squirrel who looked at me as if to say: human, there are better things to do. And I said to him: squirrel, this poem is a nut for my species. A nut and a hope that, in their bellies, it might inspire them to live a life that cares for you, and everyone you know, and everyone they know, until we all are held in the caring. A poem is both: a caring and a sharing: a caring without end; a sharing *of* ourselves, a sharing *with* another, and a sharing *in* some elemental connectivity that ties us together. These words try to honor those ties. To say to everyone they've come from, and everyone they might speak to: thank you. Thank you for being here, for being with me, for ushering these words forth, for helping me, and those around us, to survive, and more than that: to thrive. When I say us, I don't mean people. I mean the whole existential community. These poems are a thank you to the dogs and birds and trees and stones that preserve my sanity and give me heart; and they're a thank you to the Earthly condition of life by which we breathe and find ourselves able: to sense, to move, to participate in creation. They're a thank you to Mother Earth and

Grandmother Universe, whose wombs we live and die in, whose bodies we are throughout and beyond all of our myriad manifestations. These words are—at heart, in spirit— an acknowledgment *of* and appreciation *for* whatever might be honored, including you, dear reader, including you.

And including Aaron Kent, for believing in this book and believing in me and being a dream to work with. And including the editors of the following publications, who gave many of these poems their first moments in the light: David Lehman at *The American Scholar*; David Stavanger & Rebecca O'Connor at *The Moth*; Dorothy Chan at *Hobart*; Dorothy Chan & Meghan Lamb at *Sporklet*; Raena Shirali & Brittany Rogers at *Muzzle Magazine*; Cyril Wong at *Softblow*; Neil Slevin at *Dodging the Rain*; Matt Hart at *Forklift, Ohio*; Isaura Ren at *Perhappened Mag*; Sarah Katz at *Deaf Poets Society*; Alisa Golden at **82 Review*; Jason Myers & Crystal Brandt at *EcoTheo Review*; and Charlie Baylis at *Anthropocene.*

And last, but most of all, these poems are kneeling gratitudes to my deepest loves, who keep me going and fuel my fires, in verse and everything else I do: Addie, Rascal, Bonnie, Bailey and Charlie—life with you is the height of living, and my soul is a composite of pawprints where you've walked, dreams where you've snored, nose-drippings where you've sniffed, and saliva where you've licked and taught me the true deliciousness of the world; and Safora, my wife, my life— with you I learn what love is, with you I am endlessly enlightened to find that each day, no matter the immensity of its inheritance, can hold so much more than all that came before.

LAY OUT YOUR UNREST